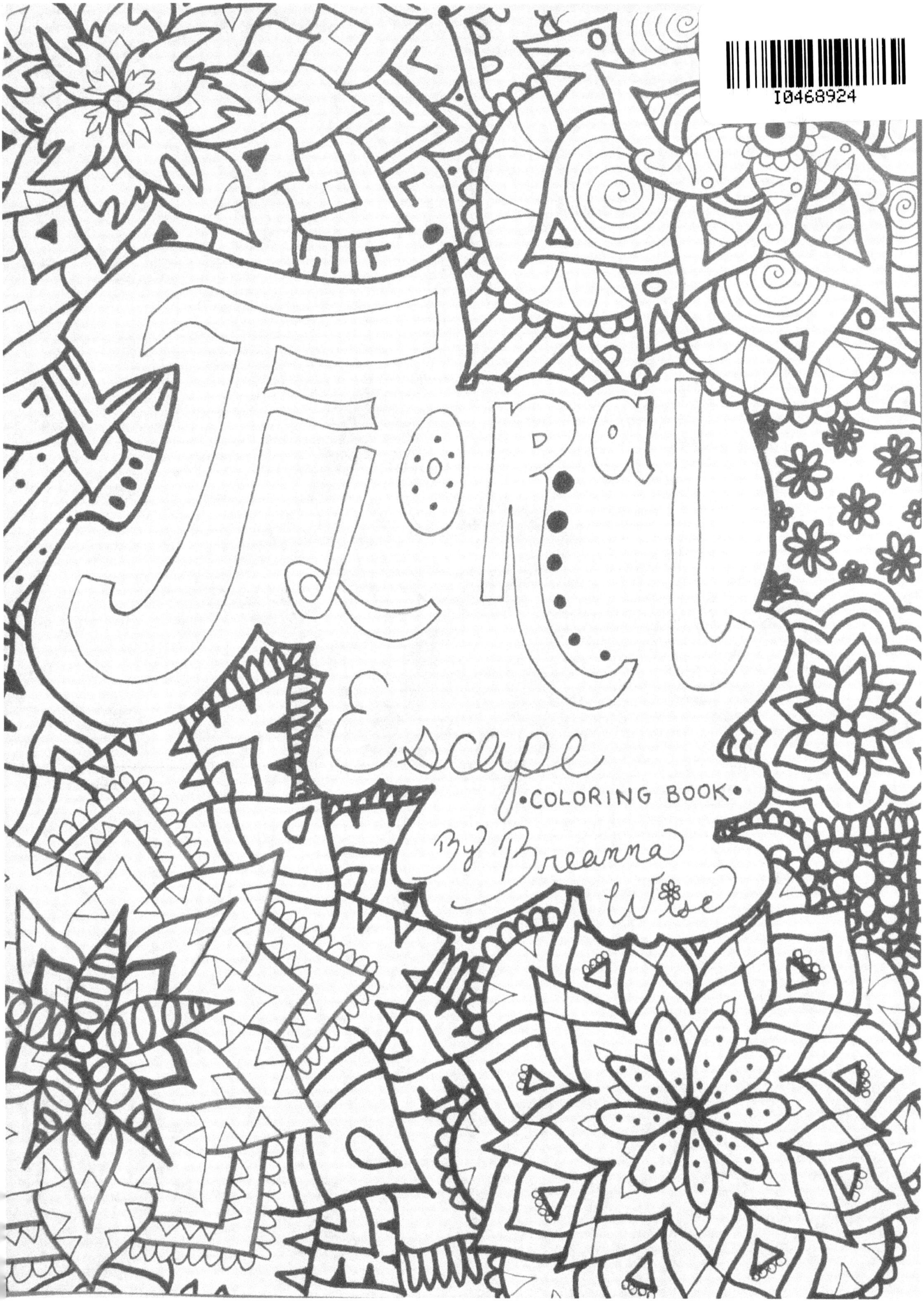
Floral
Escape
•COLORING BOOK•
By Breanna Wise

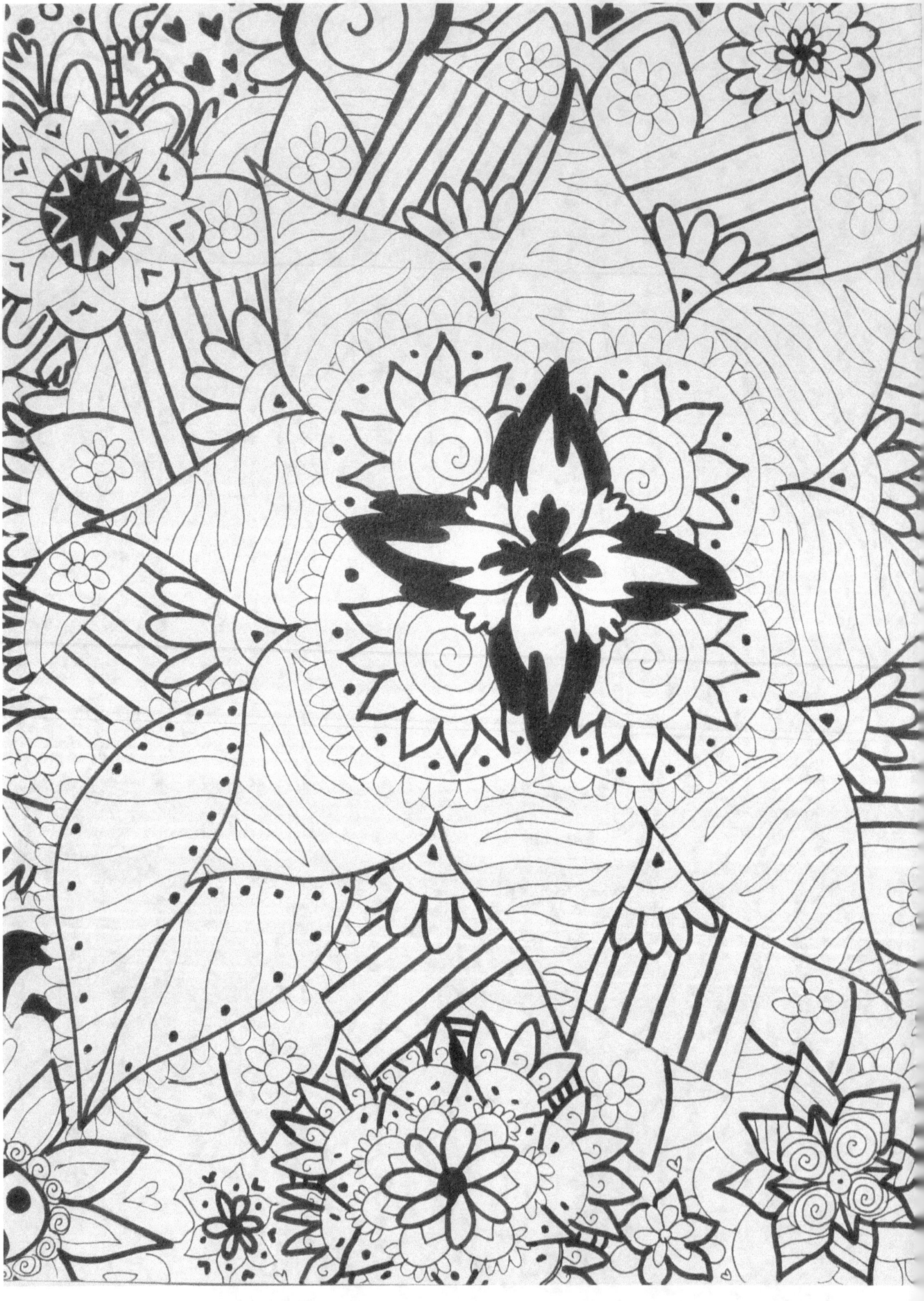

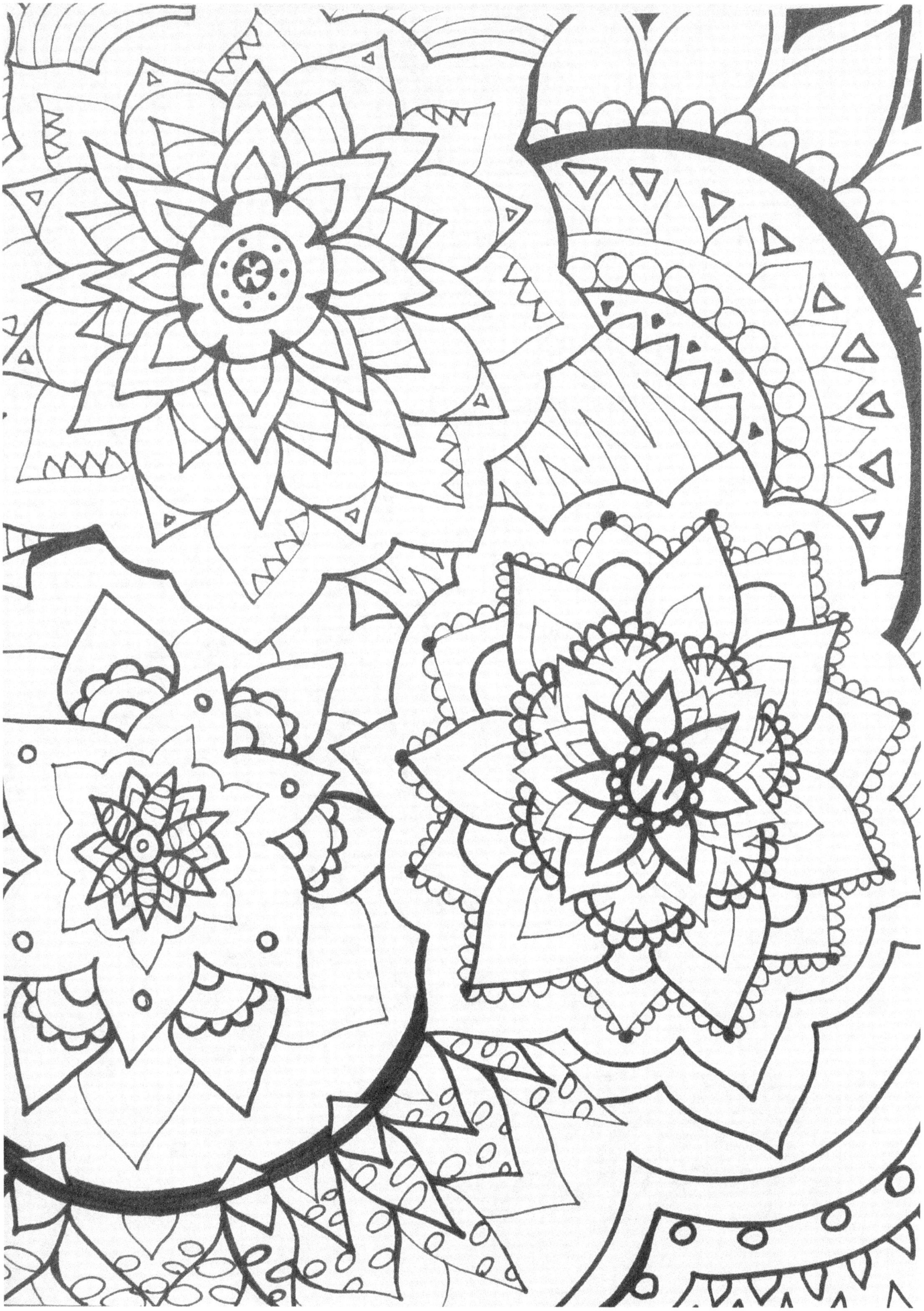

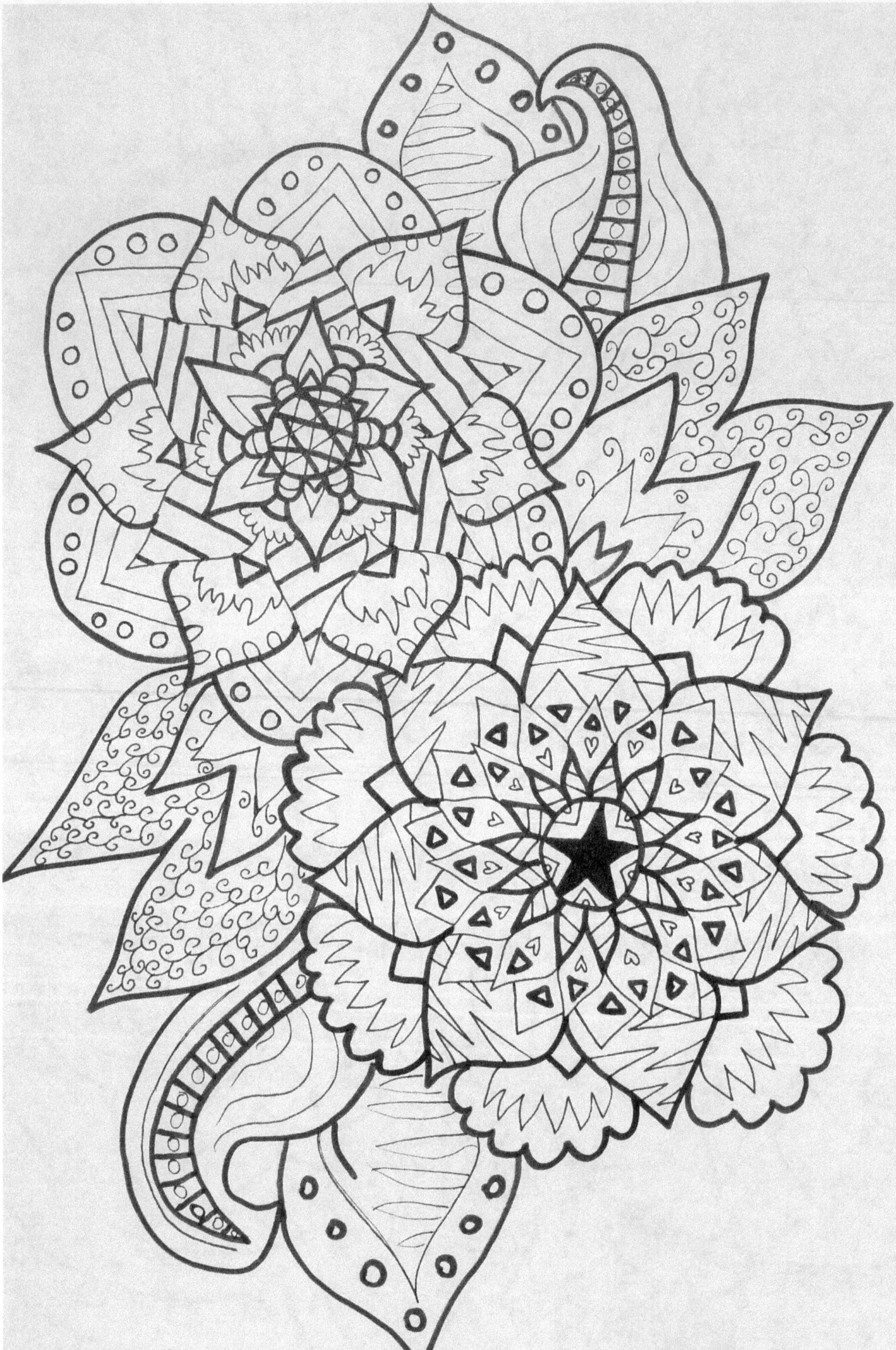

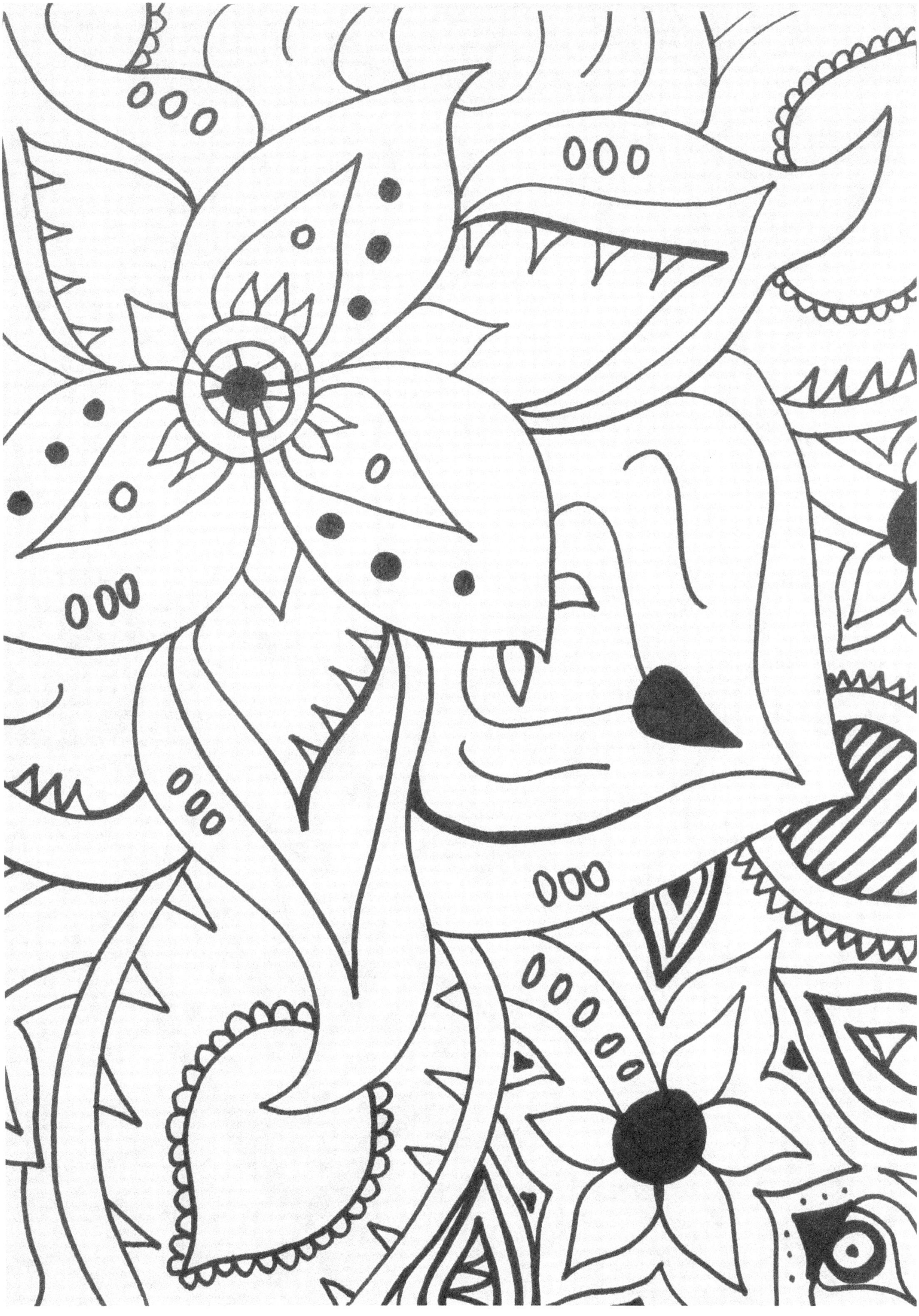

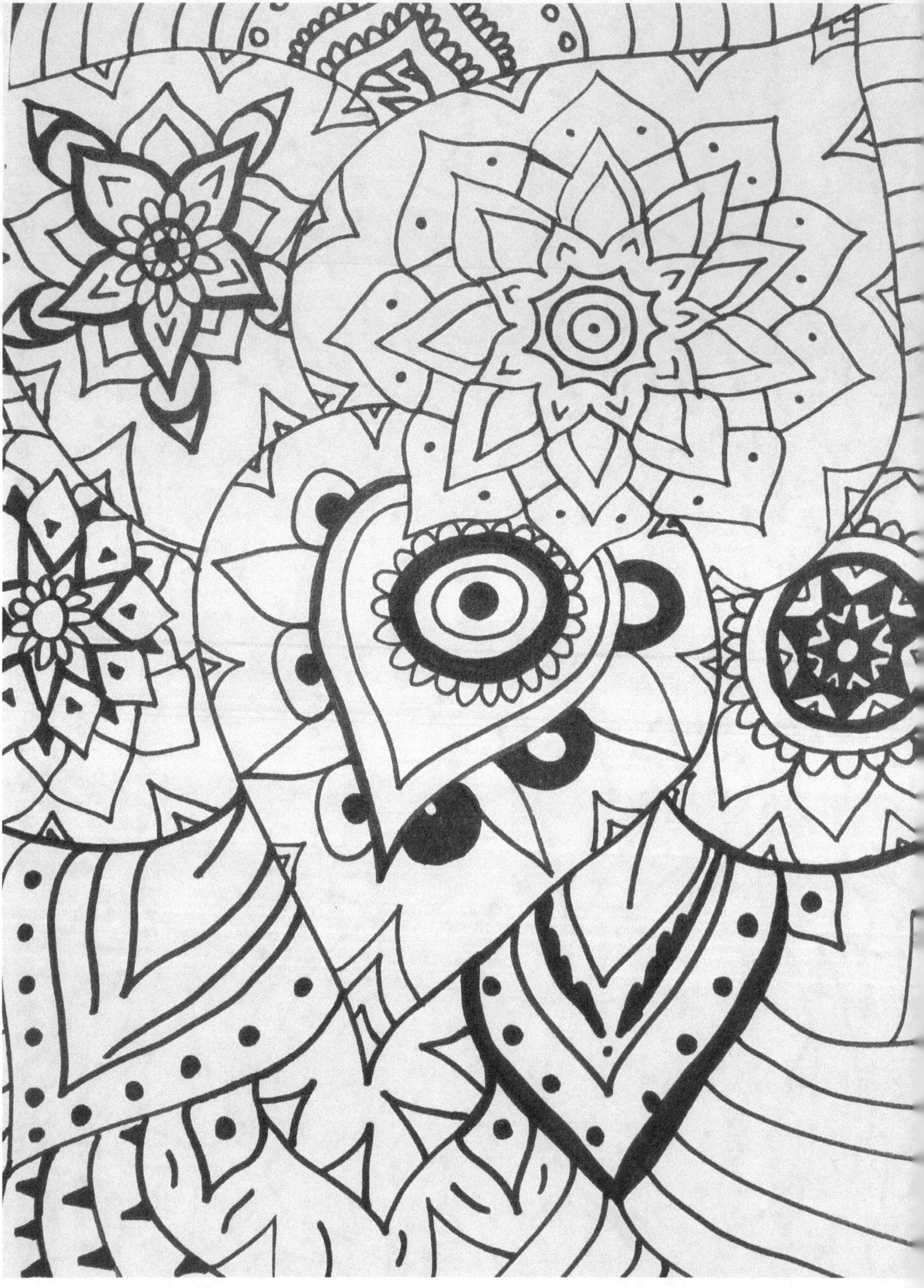

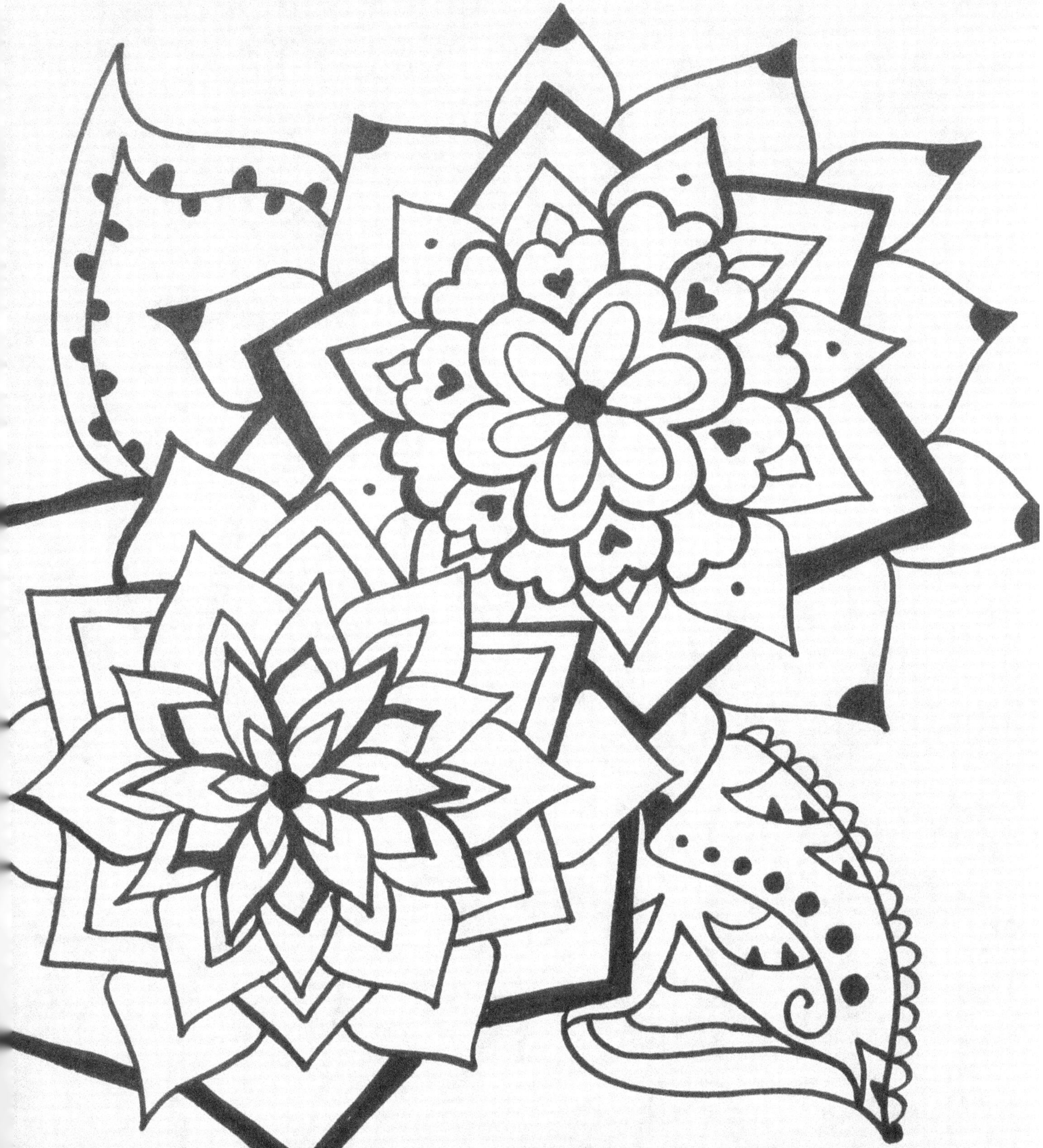

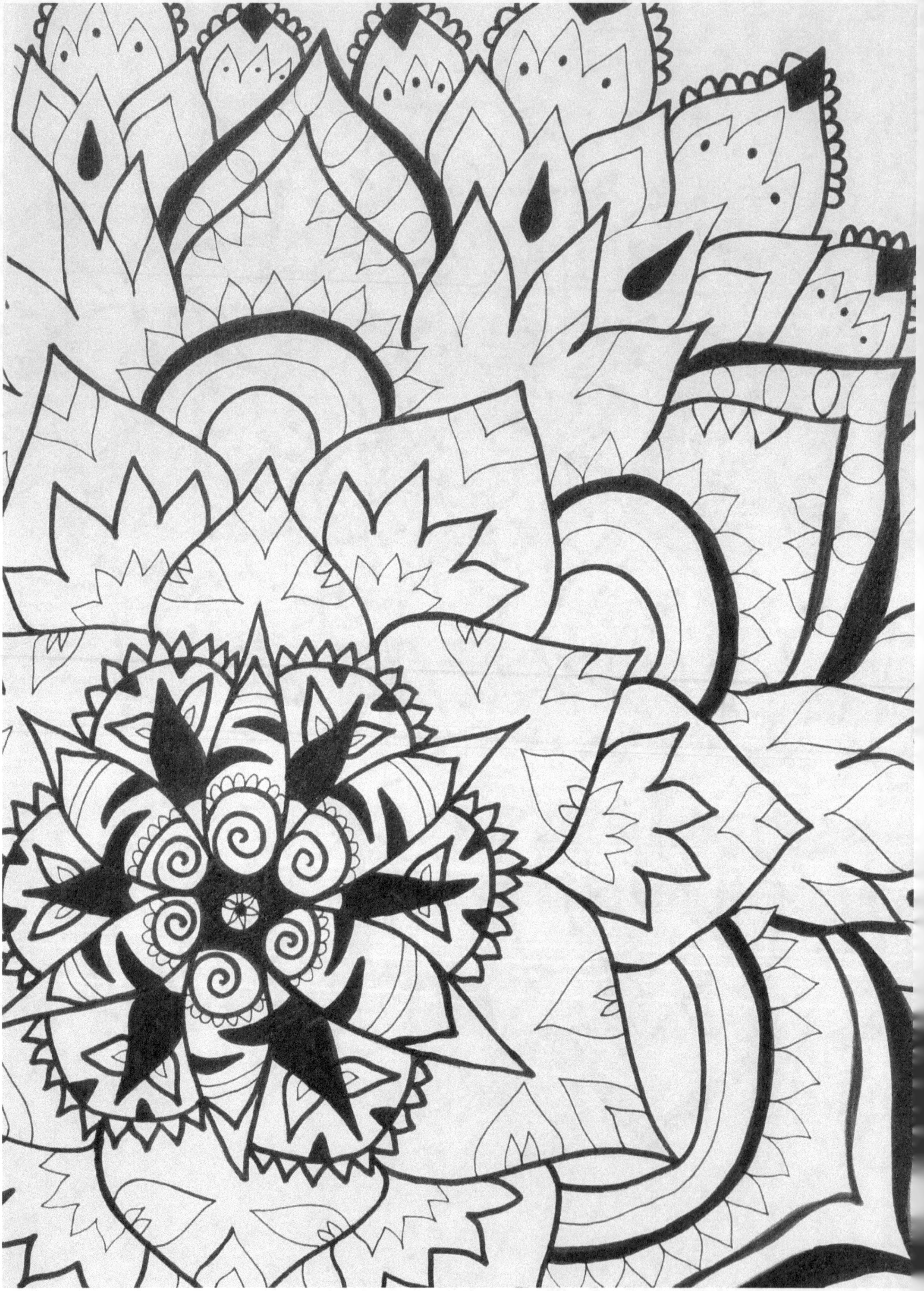

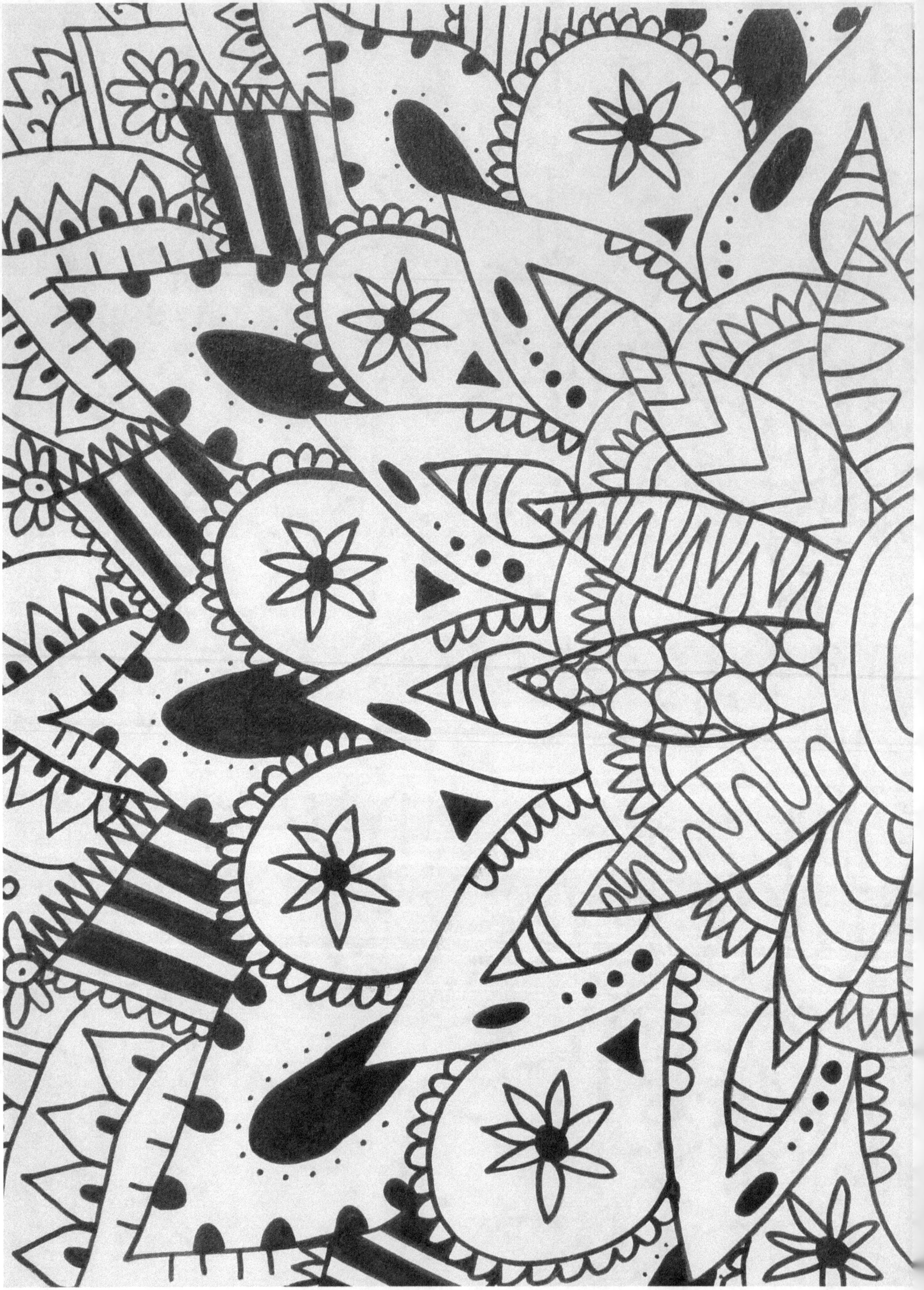

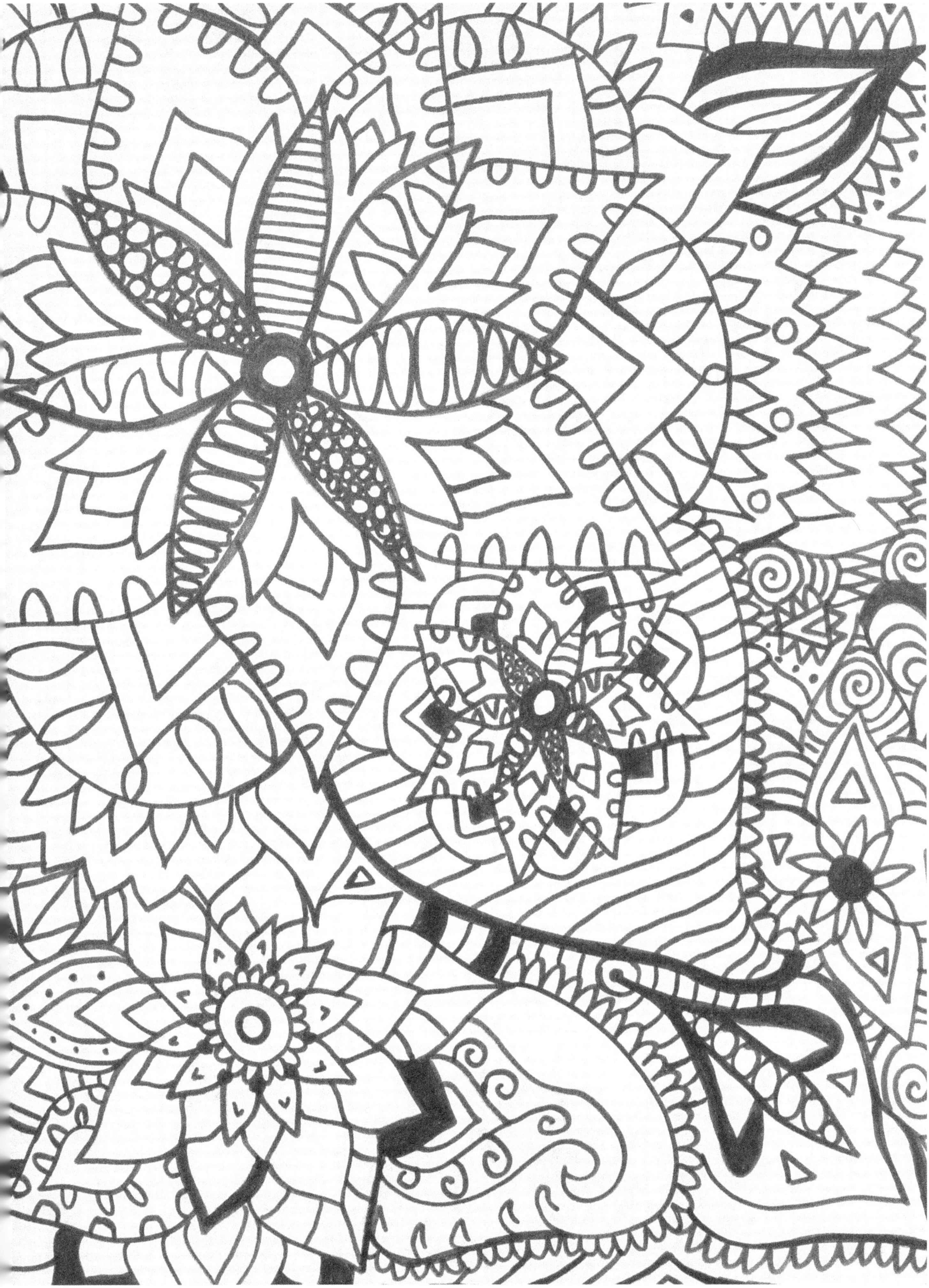

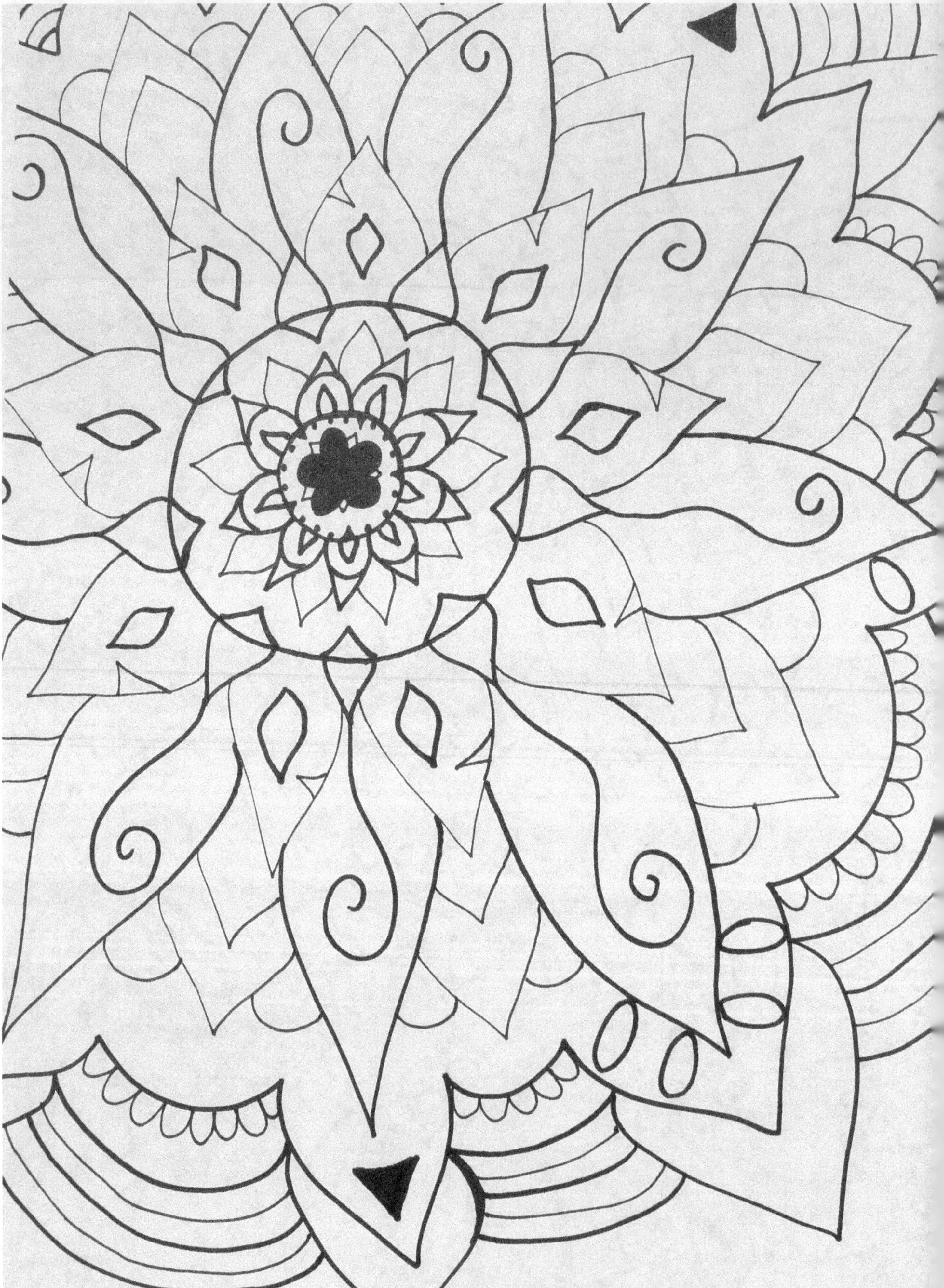

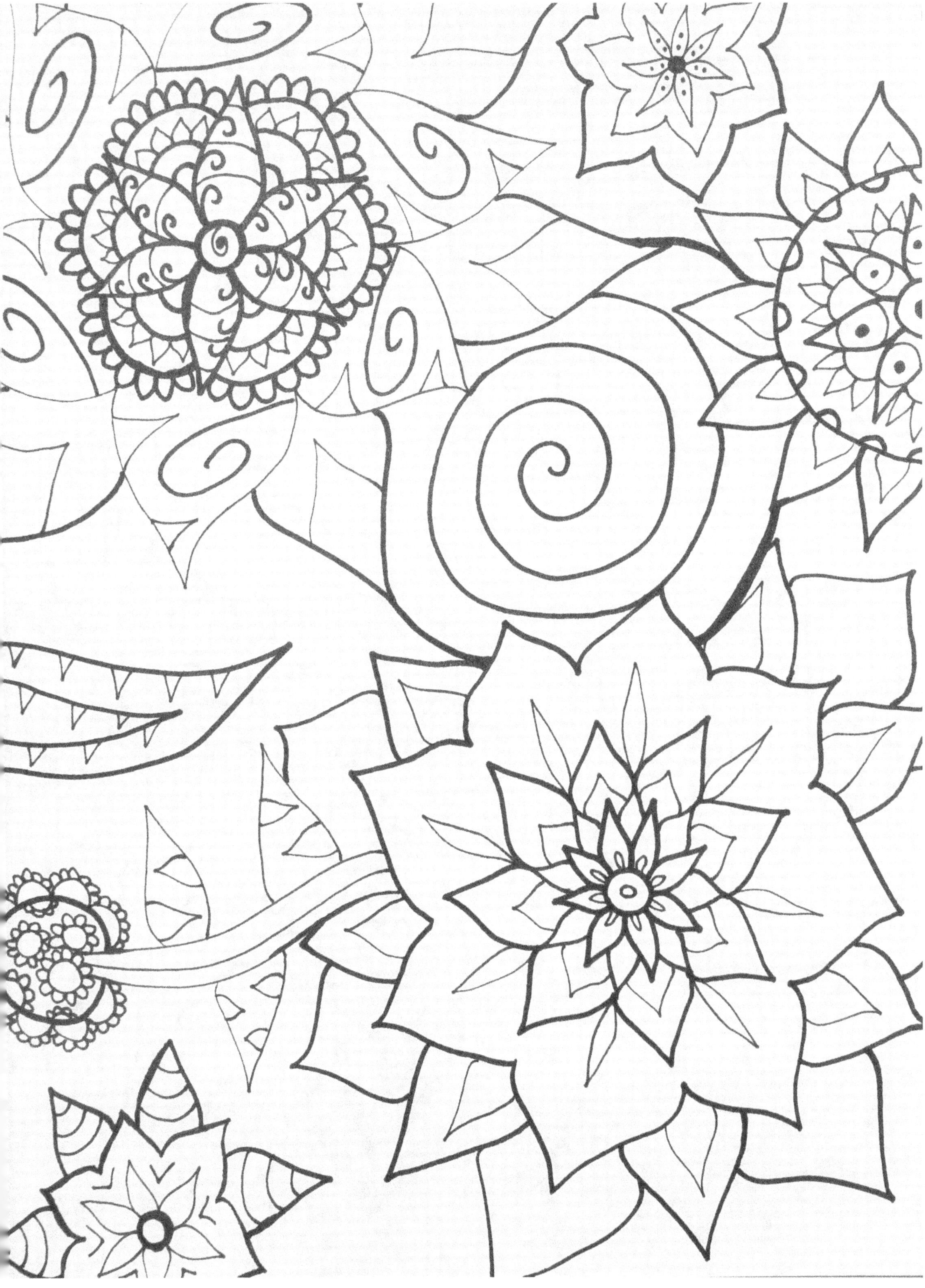

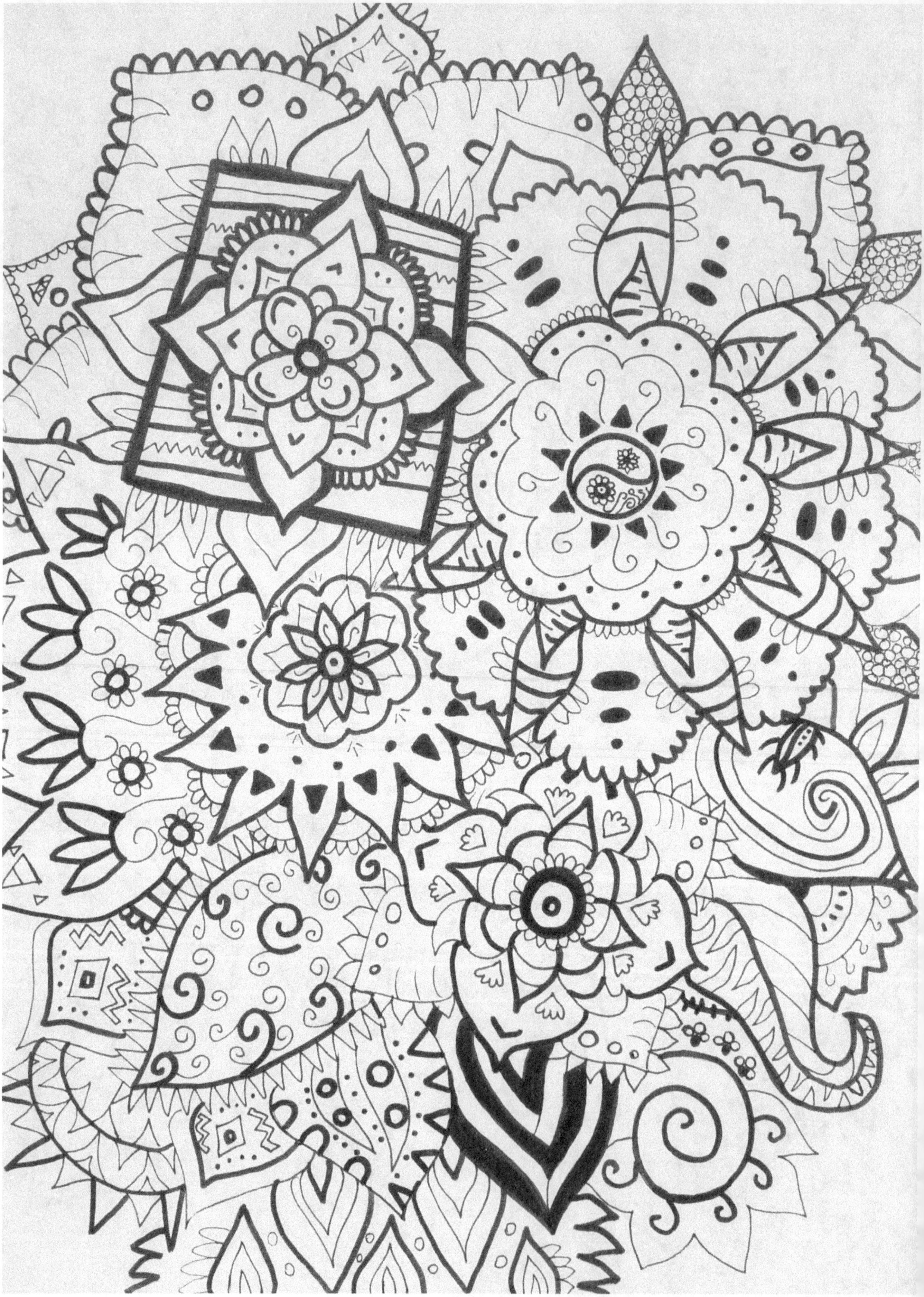

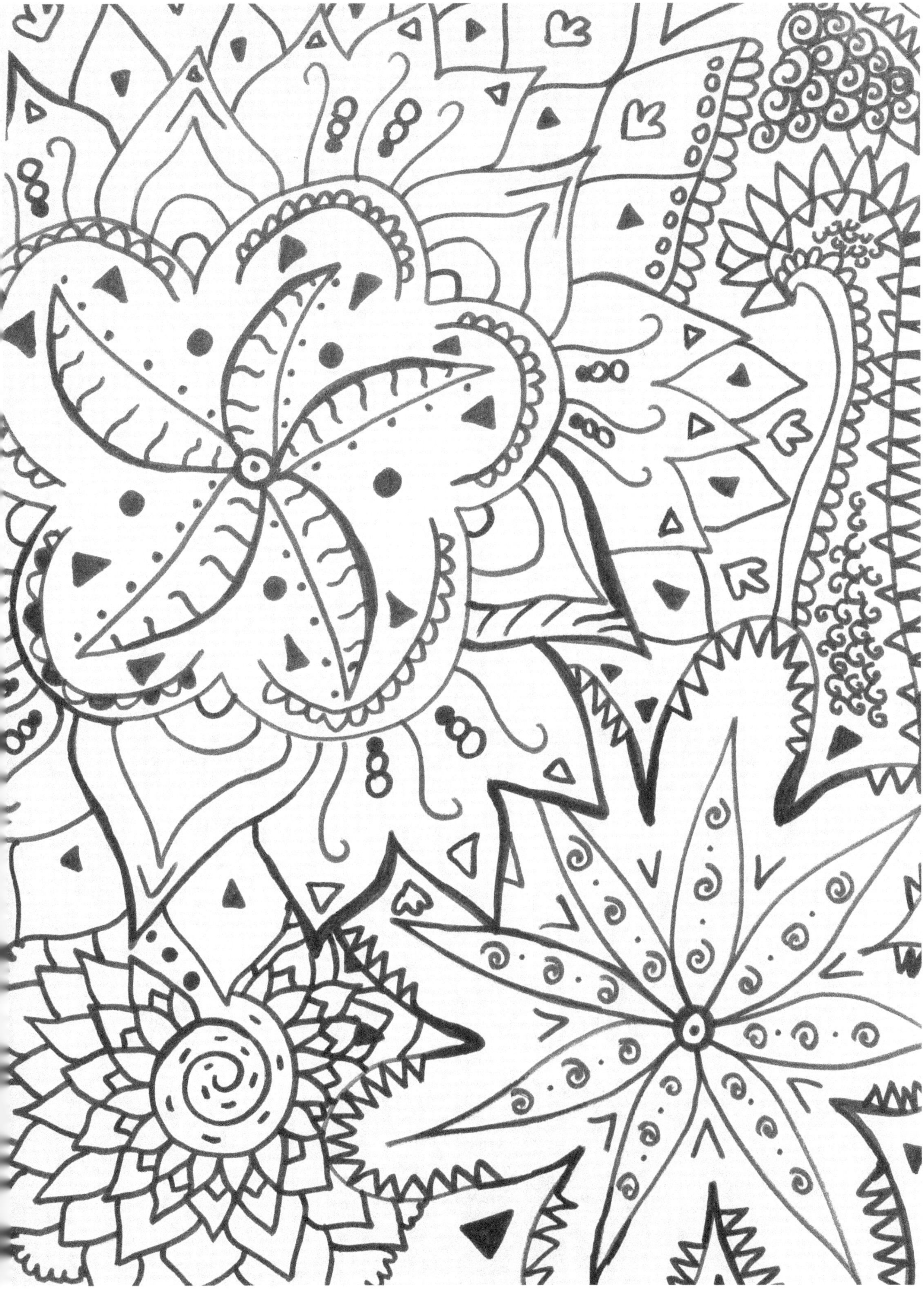

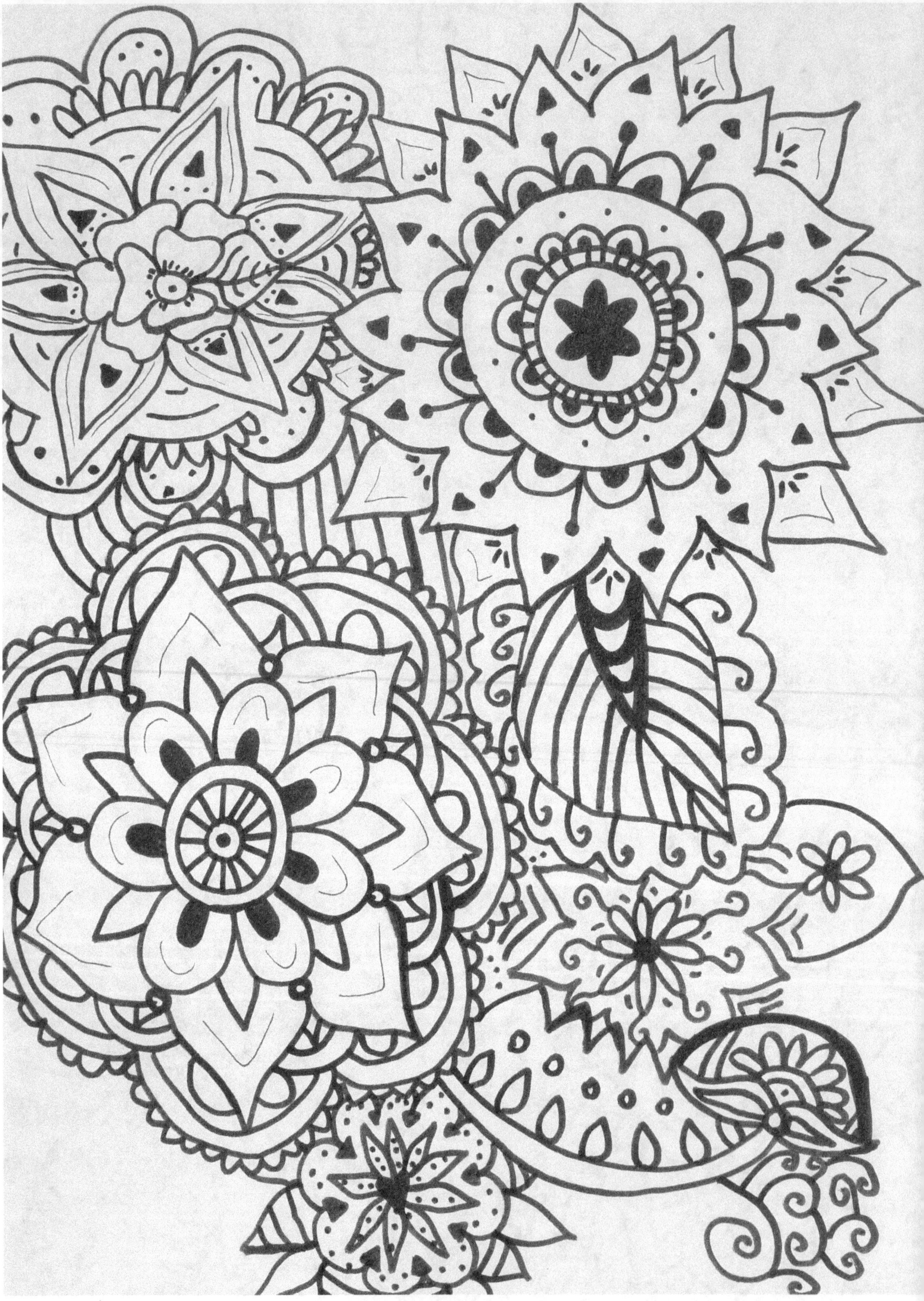

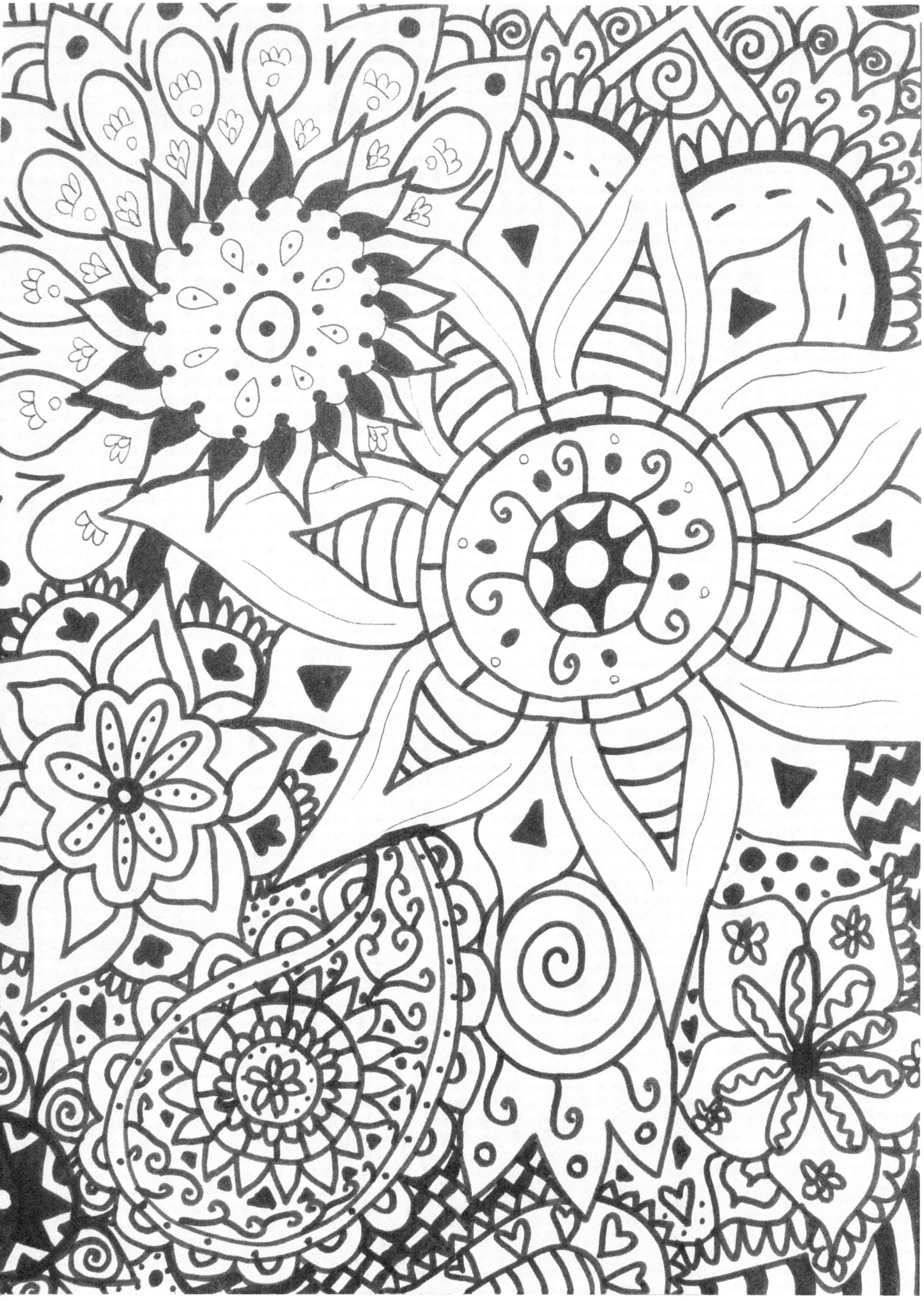

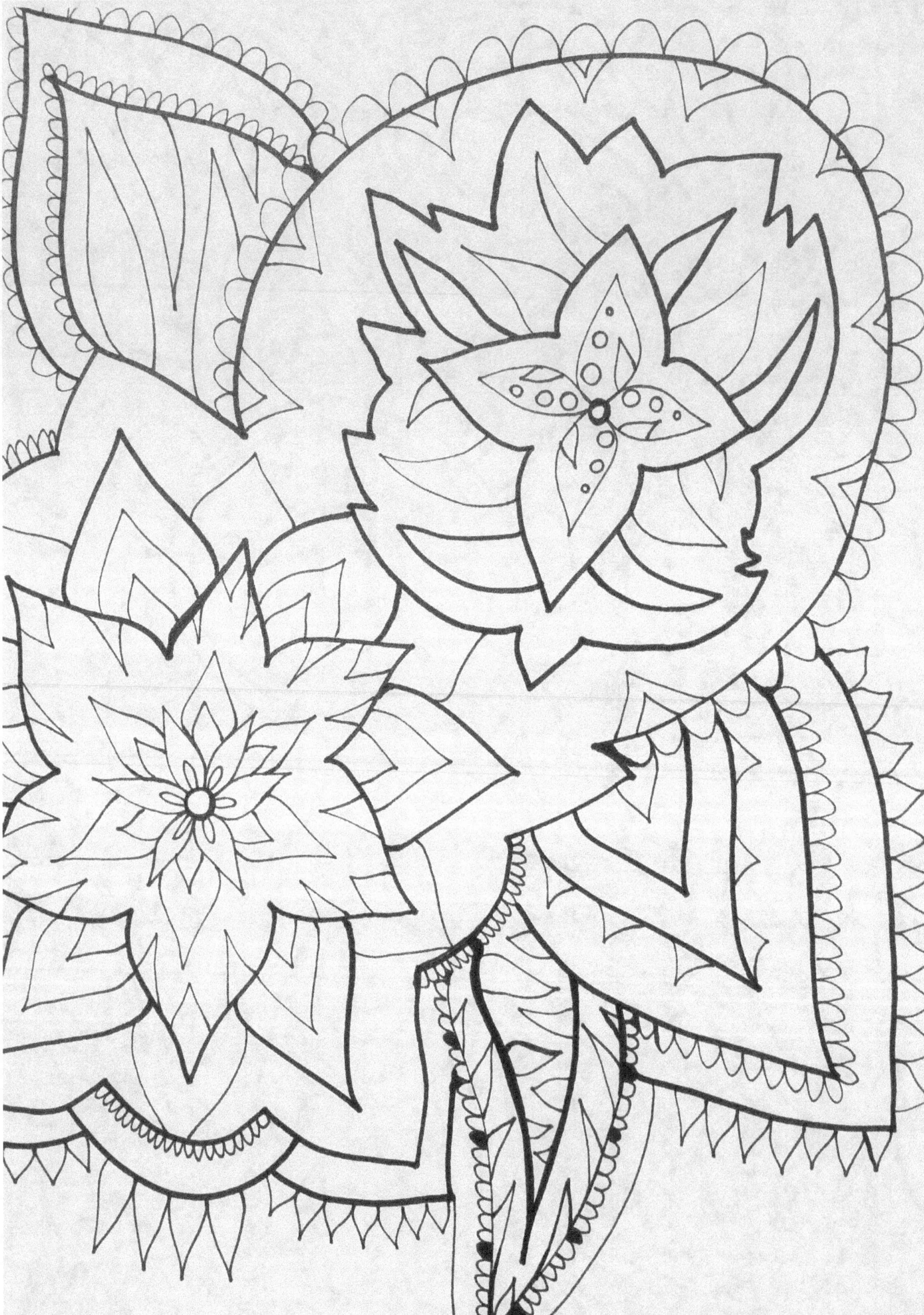

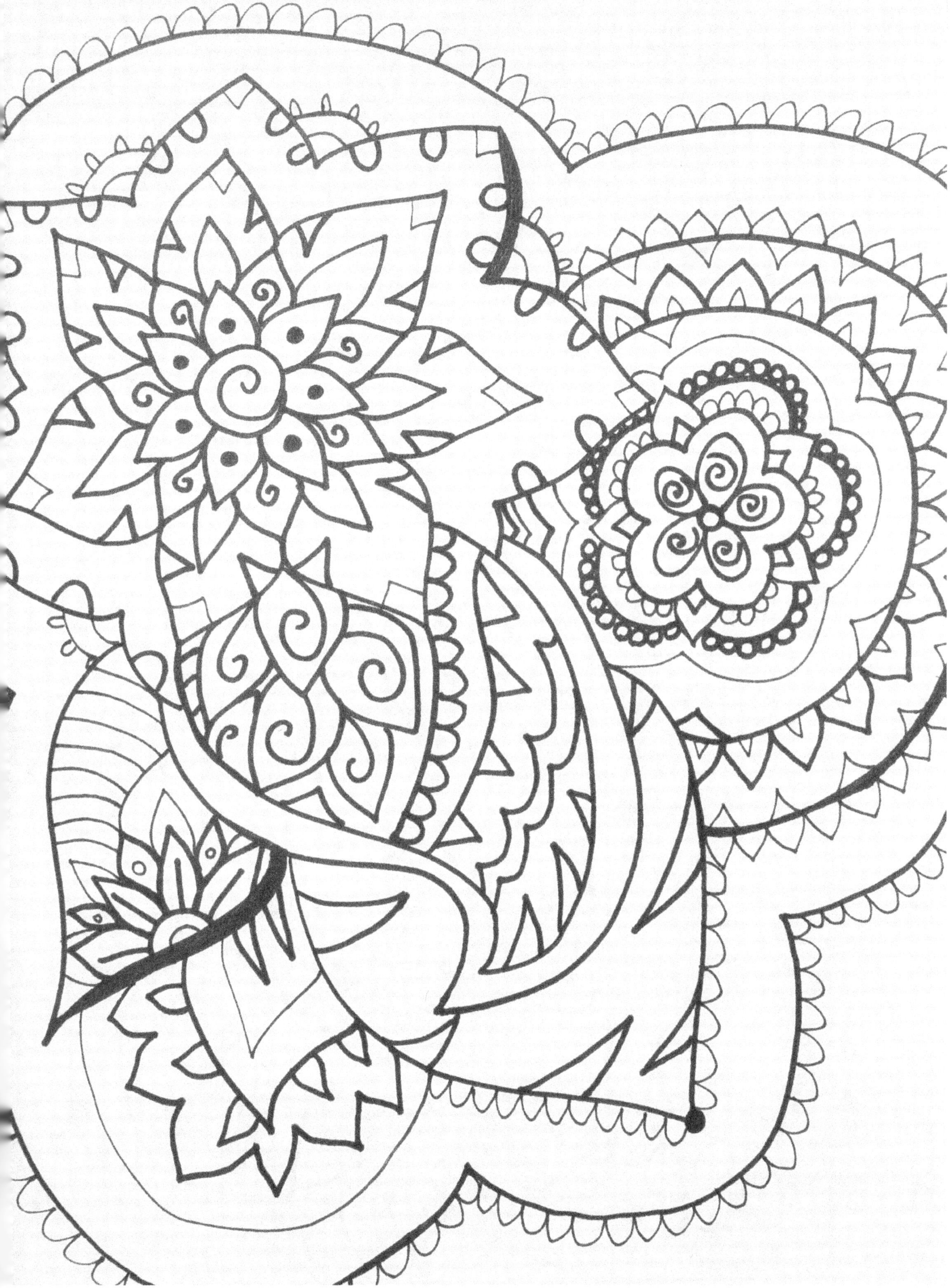

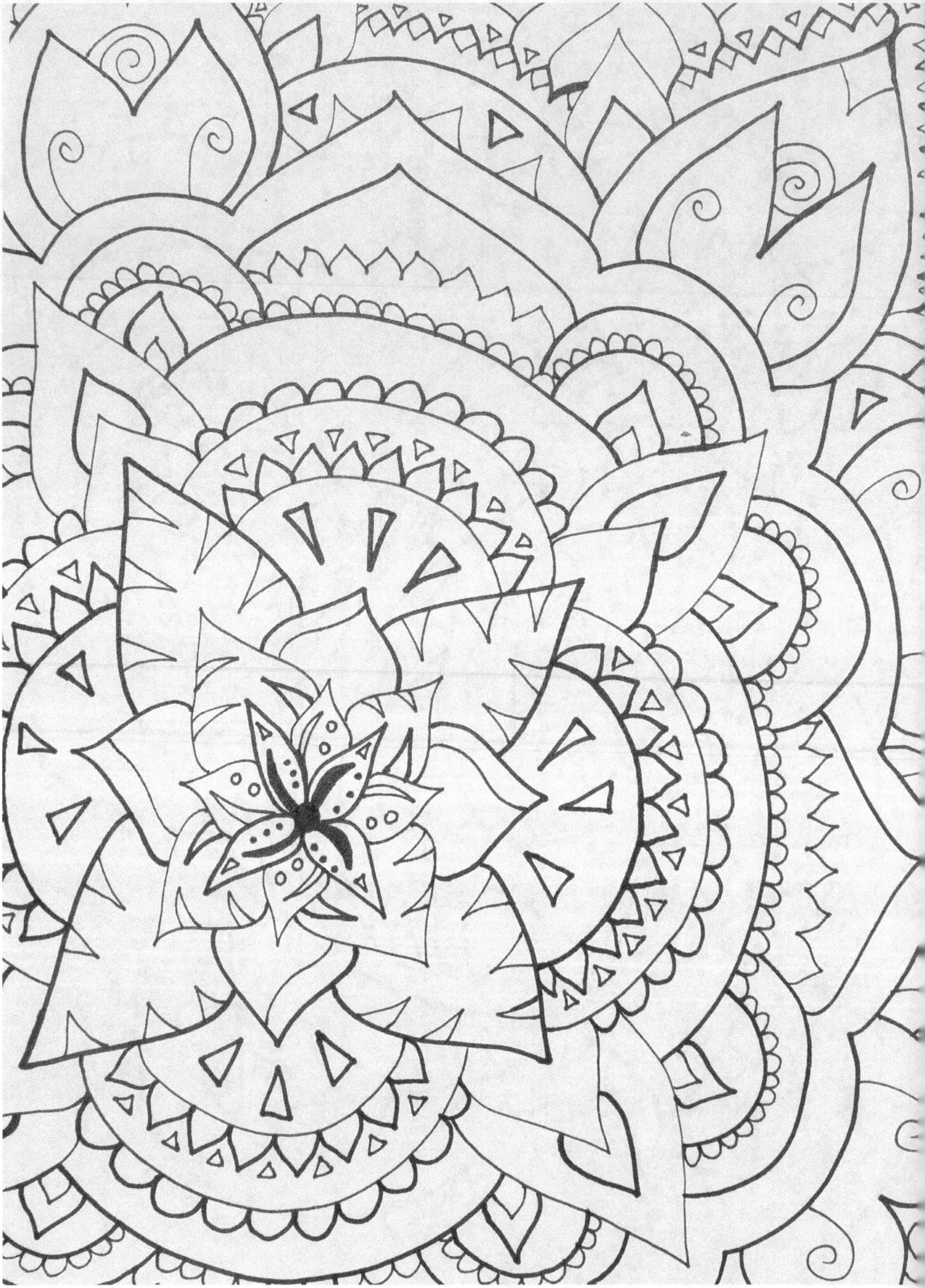

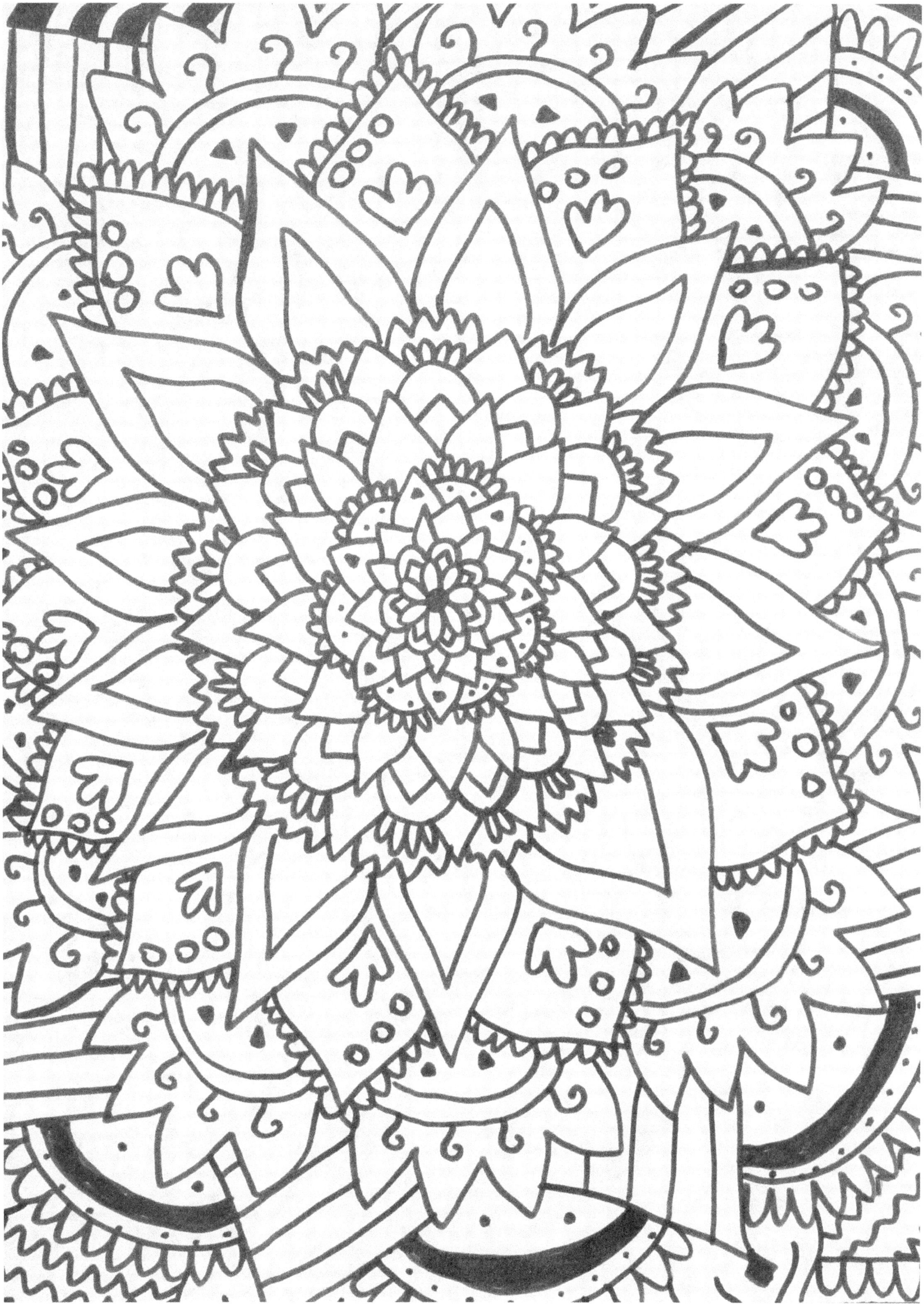

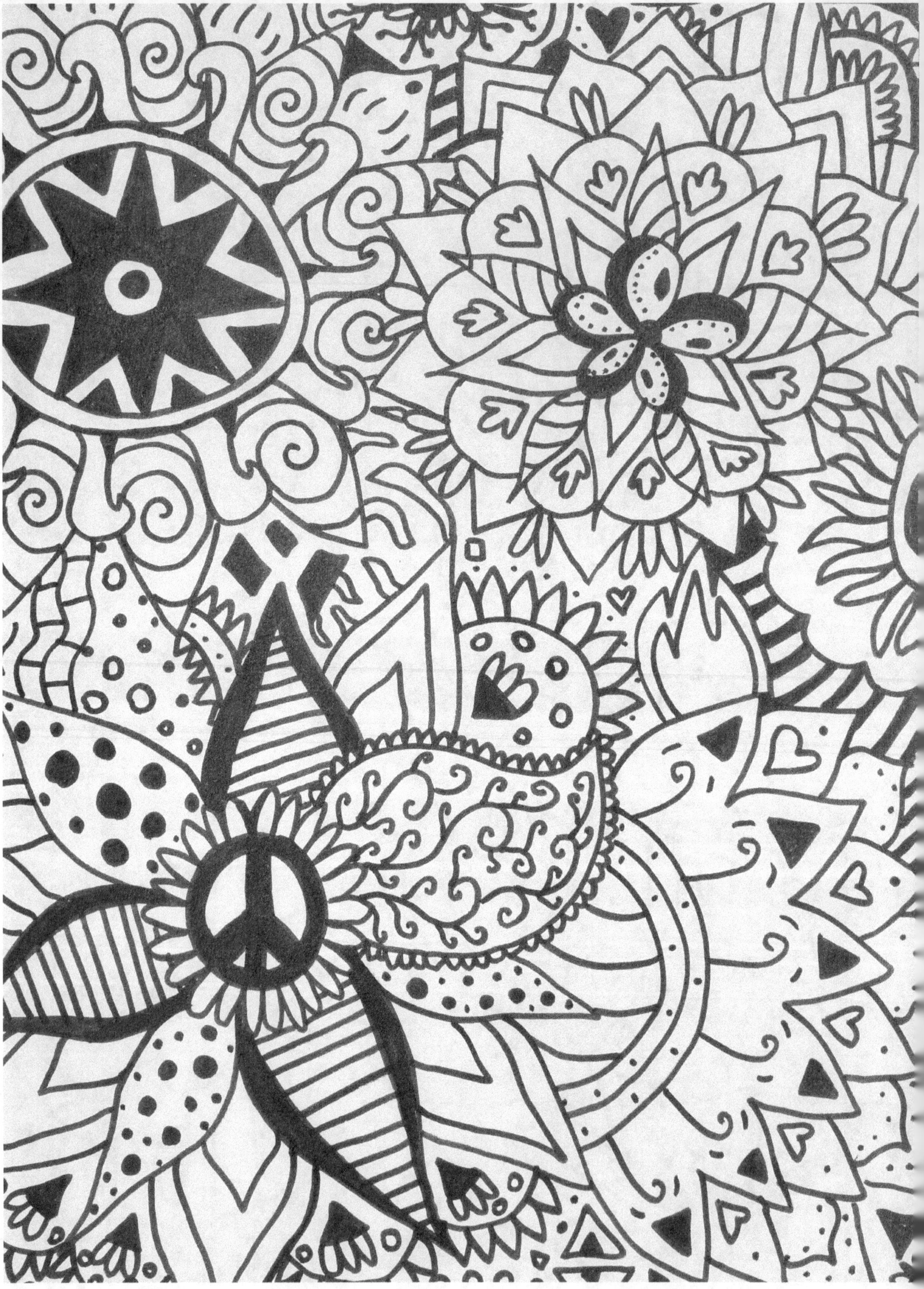

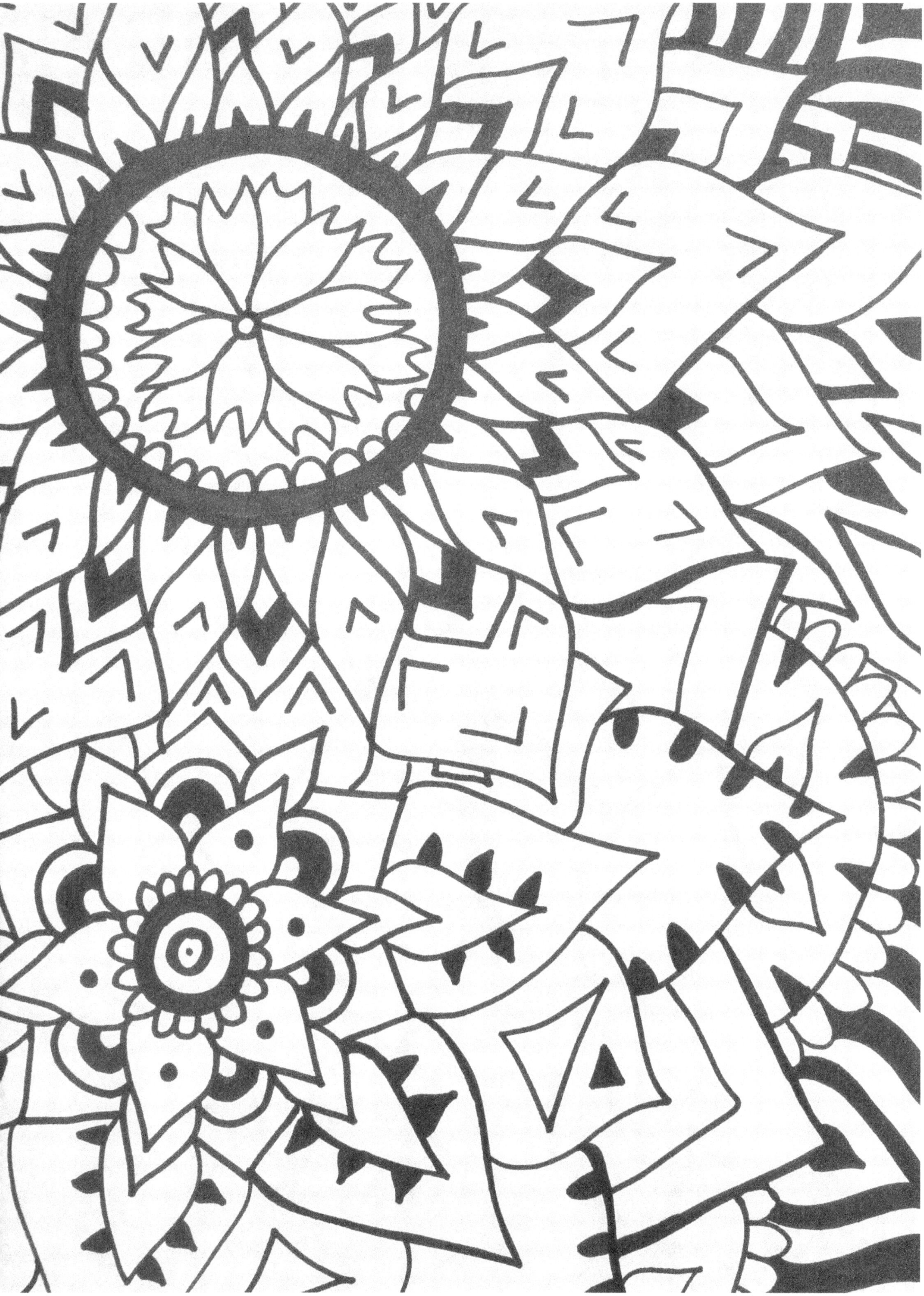

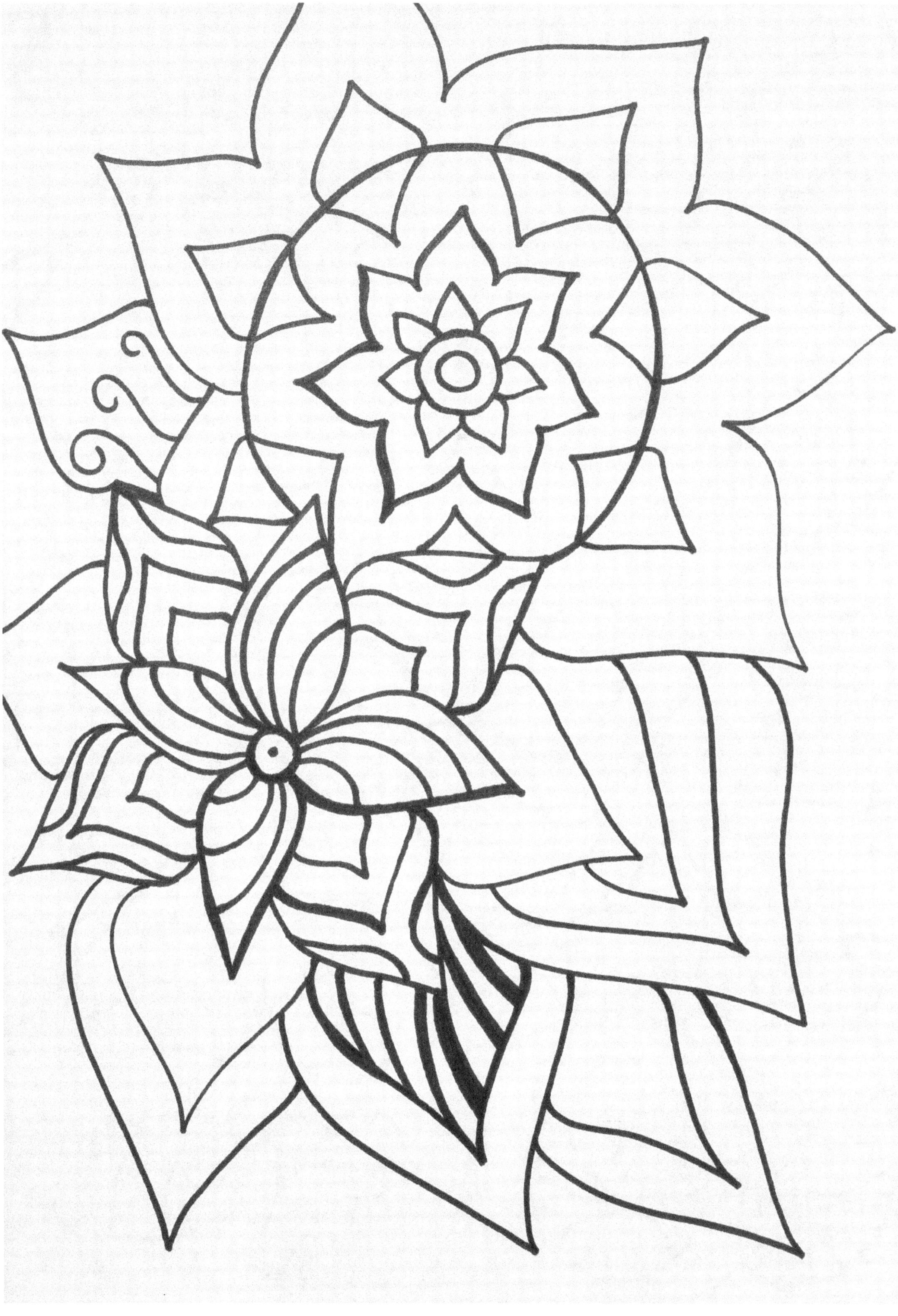

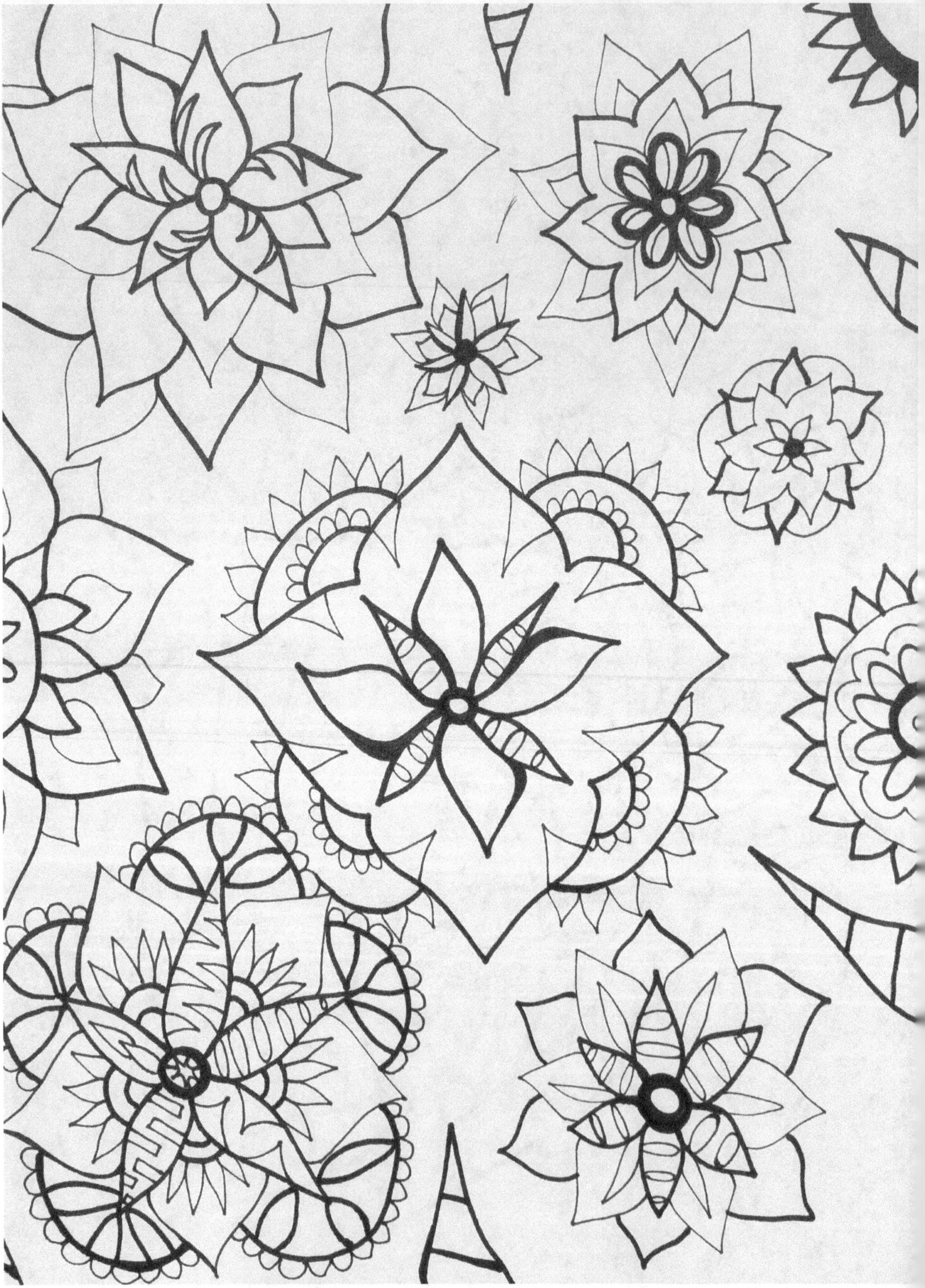

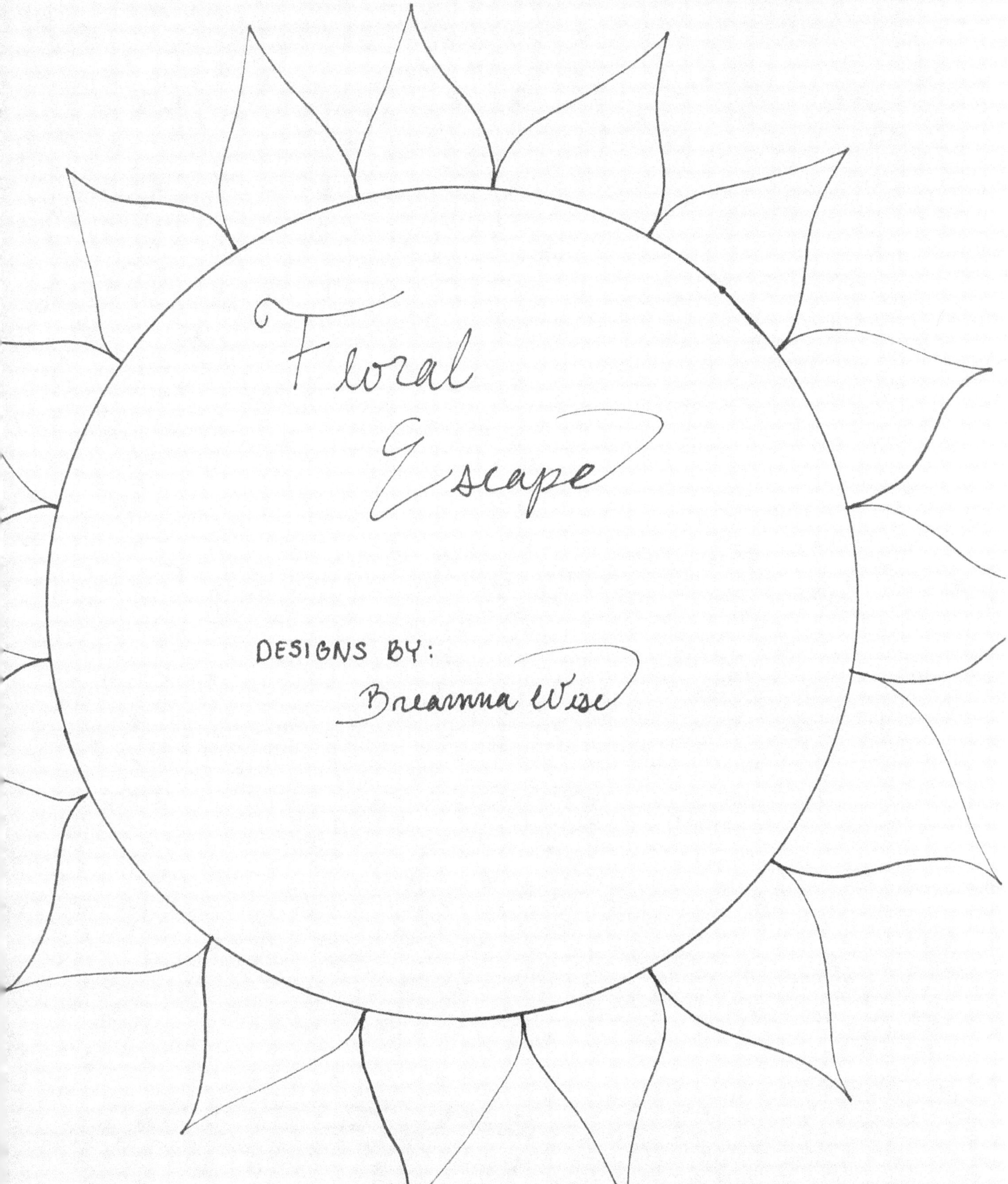
Floral Escape
DESIGNS BY:
Breanna Wise

www.ingramcontent.com/pod-product-compliance
Lightning Source LLC
Chambersburg PA
CBHW080533190526
45169CB00008B/3144
* 9 7 8 1 5 2 3 6 6 4 3 0 6 *